May Basket

Eleanor Burns

W9-BSQ-648

To Kathy, Pat, Judy, and Bruce
And our Childhood Memories of May Day

Illustrations and Paste Up by Merritt Voigtlander
Photography by Brian Steutel
Printing by A & L Litho, Escondido, CA

First Printing — May 1987
Second Printing — July 1987
Third Printing — October 1987
Fourth Printing — August 1988

Quilt in a Day ® 1955 Diamond Street, Unit A   San Marcos, CA. 92069

(619) 436-8936

Table of Contents

Introduction

I always looked forward to spring in my hometown of Zelienople, a little town heavy with German ancestry in western Pennsylvania. We usually had snow in the winter and were housebound. My sisters, Kathy, Pat, and Judy, my brother Bruce, and I all waited patiently for that fresh spring air! We looked forward to the first wild flowers popping up in the rich soil next to the Connoquenessing Creek, a small creek that quietly meandered behind the house we grew up in.

For days, we planned and made May Baskets out of colored construction paper, ribbon, and rickrack. On May 1, we were ready! Off to the creek bed we'd walk, searching for those early spring treasures. I remember the delight I always felt in discovering my first jack-in-the-pulpits standing straight and tall, bright yellow buttercups, purple violets, and sometimes, stray white violets or lily of the valley flowers.

After we'd gather the wild flowers and carefully fill the baskets, we would hang them on the door knobs of our favorite neighbors, ring the door bell, and run, giggling all the while! Each year we couldn't wait to repeat this May Day tradition! Our neighbors looked forward to the "little Knoechel kids" and their adventure.

I love these memories of my childhood and I love to share these "little girl stories" with my sons, Grant and Orion. To me, making a quilt for someone you love is like making a May Day tradition, a memory to hold onto forever! I want you to feel that same "girlish warmth" as you make your own quilt.

Because I know your life is as full of "family traditions" as mine is, I wanted your May Basket quilt to sew up quickly and easily. In my early technique development stage, Orion stood beside me with his stop watch as I tried different approaches. The quick pressing method I settled on is as much a time saver as the sewing method.

So don't become a "Basket Case!"
Make a "tradition" instead!

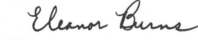

Materials and Supplies

Fabric

Select a good quality of 100% cotton 45" wide for your blocks and backing. If you wish, prewash the lights and darks separately with soap in a gentle wash cycle. If you do not prewash your fabric before making your quilt, carefully hand wash it in cold water with a delicate soap.

Batting

Select bonded polyester batting for the inside of your quilt in your choice of thicknesses. The thickest battings, 8 oz. – 10 oz., show the most dimension when tied and are the warmest. A thin batting, 2 – 3 oz., is the best for hand or machine quilting. Check for a brand of bonded batting that has not been treated with formaldehyde and has no "needle drag." It should feel soft to the touch and not fall apart when tugged on. If you are going to "stitch in the ditch" through the borders, practice on various pieces of batting sandwiched between two pieces of fabric to find the best thickness.

Floss

Use all strands of embroidery floss, crochet thread, pearl cotton, candlewicking yarn, or 100% wool yarn for tying down the blocks. To test the durability of a fiber, hold several strands between your fingers and rub the ends briskly. Don't use yarns or fibers that fray easily. Purchase three packages of floss for sizes up to twin, and six packages for sizes up to king.

Lace (Optional)

Select a ruffled lace or ruffled cluny 3/4" wide for trimming the basket, and 1 1/2" wide for trimming the ruffle around the outside edge of the quilt. Since ruffled eyelet tends to stretch the basket during sewing, you may wish to choose a flat eyelet. Consider buying just a small amount of lace and sewing with it before buying all the yardage. Ribbon can be easily threaded through cluny lace.

Ribbon (Optional)

Each basket uses two 12" pieces of 1/4" satin ribbon run through cluny lace with a wide-eyed needle. Purchase this much ribbon for your particular quilt:

Baby...... 2 3/4 yards	Double.......13 1/2 yards
Lap..............4 yards	Queen .... 16 yards
Twin.............10 yards	King .... 20 yards

Thread

Purchase a large spool of polyester spun thread in a neutral shade, plus a large spool of thread to match the backing color.

Color Selection
and Variations

Select dark for the basket, light for the background color, and medium for the solid square. As a variation, the basket could be light with the background color dark.

Vary the scales of your prints: use a large scale print, a small scale print, and a solid or one that looks like a solid. A large scale print is extremely attractive used as the basket and handle, the solid colored fabric as the background, and the small scale print as the square in between the basket blocks. For a variation, do just the opposite and use a small scale print for the basket and a large scale print for the solid square.

Quilt of Many Colors

Yardages are given for baskets all one color. To make the baskets a variety of colors, follow the Pillows Yardage Chart on page 10. Divide the number of basket blocks in your size quilt by 2 to find how many sets of yardage you must buy. For instance, a lap robe has 6 blocks. Purchase 3 different sets of colors for 2 baskets of each color.

Quilt of Two Colors

The background color and the solid square color could be the same. In that situation, you basically see only baskets, and all other pieces blend together.

Victorian Quilt

Use a large scaled print with lace accents in both the basket and ruffle. Use eyelet yardage as the background and run ribbon through the ruffled cluny in the basket for a feminine look.

Amish Quilt

For a masculine or Amish look in a Basket Quilt, select light, medium, and dark solid colors and use them in any placement. For example, the basket may be red, the background grey, and the solid square black. Using a variety of colors in the basket is extremely attractive, as shades of blues and purples along with the same grey background and black. Consider using many shades of baskets with only a black background and solid squares.

Basket with Different Colored Handles

Using the Cutting Charts for each particular quilt, purchase the total amount needed for the handles only and deduct that amount from the basket yardage. For instance, the lap robe needs 9" for the handle. Purchase 1/4 yd. for the handle, and deduct 1/4 yd. from the basket color.

Paste Up Sheet

Make copies of the Paste Up Sheet on page 7. Paste in fabric swatches of your selection to visualize how your block will look.

Sample Paste Up Block

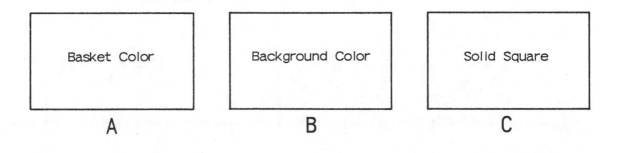

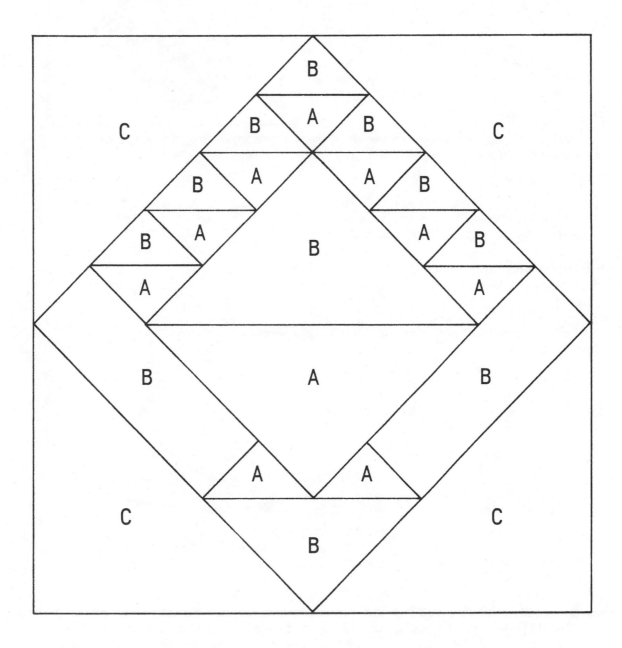

Cutting Supplies and Instruction

Use a large industrial size rotary cutter capable of cutting through several layers of fabric at one time with a plexiglas ruler on a special plastic mat. Use either a thick 6" x 12" or 6" x 24" see-thru ruler for accurately measuring and cutting strips, or a 12" square ruler for cutting both strips and squares.

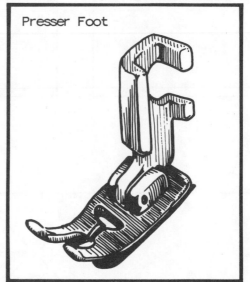
Presser Foot

Pins

Use extra-long 1 3/4" sharp pins with the colored heads for pinning, a curved upholstery needle for tying, and large safety pins for machine quilting.

Presser Foot

Use a general purpose presser foot as illustrated. Use the edge of the foot as a guide for a generous 1/4" seam allowance.

Walking Foot (Optional)

An even feed foot, or walking foot, is a useful aid while machine quilting. With the walking foot, two layers of fabric move together while being sewn and do not shift and become distorted.

Bicycle Clips

Wrap bicycle clips around a tightly rolled quilt when machine quilting.

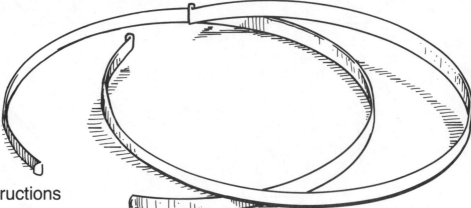

Cutting Instructions

Tear your fabric to put it on the straight of the grain by cutting a 1/2" nick into the selvage edge about 1" from the edge. Tear from one selvage to the other. If you don't get a straight edge, nick and tear again until you do.

Fold the fabric in fourths from selvage to selvage, matching up the torn straight edge. It is sometimes impossible to match up the selvage sides.

Lay your fabric on the board with most of it laying off to the right. Place the see-thru ruler on the very edge of the fabric on the left. With your left hand, firmly hold the ruler.

With the rotary cutter in your right hand, begin cutting with the blade off the fabric on the mat. Put all of your strength into the rotary cutter as you cut away from you and trim off the torn ragged edge.

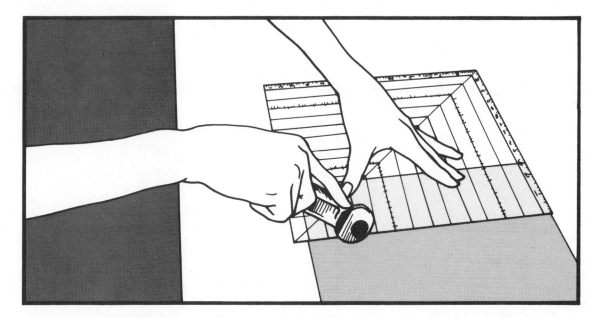

Move your ruler over, measuring and cutting the strips carefully and accurately from selvage to selvage. All strips will vary in widths but all will be approximately 45" long. All strips can then be cut easily into squares with a 12" square ruler.

If you are left-handed, reverse the cutting process with the fabric on the left and the ruler on the right.

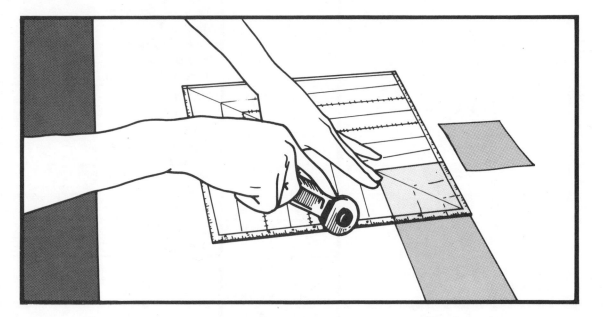

Yardage and Cutting Charts

	Yardage	Cutting
Pillows Basket Color	5/8 Yard	**Handles** One 6" x 12" Strip **Feet** Two 3" Squares **Basket** One 7" Square **Borders** Four 2 1/2" Strips
Background Color	1/4 Yard	**Handles** One 6" x 12" Strip **Basket** One 7" Square **Sides** Four 2 5/8" x 6 1/2" Strips **Bottom** One 5" Square
Solid Square Color Fabric Ruffle Backing	1/2 Yard 1 1/4 Yards 5/8 Yard	Two 12" Squares Eight 6" Strips Cut when block completed.
Lace for Ruffle Lace for Basket Bonded Batting Polyester Stuffing	10 Yards 5/8 Yard 1/2 Yard 2 Bags	 Two 18" Pieces

	Yardage	Cutting
Pillow Sham Basket Color	1/2 Yard	**Handles** One 6" x 12" Strip **Feet** Two 3" Squares **Basket** One 7" Square **Borders** Three 3" Strips
Background Color	1/4 Yard	**Handles** One 6" x 12" Strip **Basket** One 7" Sqaure **Sides** Four 2 5/8" x 6 1/2" **Bottom** One 5" Square
Solid Square Color	1/2 Yard	One 12" Square One 16 1/2" Square
Fabric Ruffle Backing Lace for Ruffle Lace for Basket Bonded Batting	1 Yard 5/8 Yard 6 1/2 Yards 5/8 Yard 5/8 Yard	Five 6" Strips

Wallhanging

	Yardage	Cutting
Basket Color	1 Yard	**Handle** One 9" Square **Basket** One 11 1/2" Square **Feet** One 4 1/2" Square **Corner Patches** One 9" x 18" Strip **Border** Four 4" Strips
Background Color	1 Yard	**Handle** One 9" Square **Basket** One 11 1/2" Square **Sides** Two 4" x 11 1/2" Strips **Bottom** One 8" Square **Border** Four 4" Strips
Solid Square Color	5/8 Yard	**Corner Triangles** One 19 3/4" Square **Corner Patches** One 9" x 18" Strip
Lace for Basket Backing Lightweight Batting	1/2 Yard 1 1/4 Yards 44" Square	

Baby Quilt

	Blocks	Borders
	Four Baskets	
Basket Color	1/2 Yard	1/2 Yard
Background Color	2/3 Yard	2/3 Yard
Solid Square Color	1/2 Yard	
Fabric Ruffle	(Optional)	1 1/2 Yards
Lace for Ruffle		10 Yards
Lace for Basket		1 1/4 Yards
Backing		1 1/4 Yards
Bonded Batting		45" Square
Approximate Finished Size		43" x 43"

Cutting Chart

Check off and label as pieces are cut.

	Blocks	Borders
Basket Color	**Handles** ☐ One 9" Strip **Feet** ☐ Four 3" Squares **Basket** Cut later when first handle is completed.	(4) 3 1/2" Strips
Background Color	**Handles** ☐ One 9" Strip **Sides** ☐ Two 2 5/8" Strips **Bottom** ☐ Two 5" Squares **Basket** Cut later when first handle is completed.	(4) 4 1/2" Strips
Solid Square Color	Cut later when basket block is completed.	
Fabric Ruffle		(8) 6" Strips
Backing		45" Square

Lap Robe

Blocks

	Six Baskets	Borders
Basket Color	1/2 Yard	5/8 Yard
Background Color	2/3 Yard	7/8 Yard
Solid Square Color	7/8 Yard	
Fabric Ruffle		1 3/4 Yards
Lace for Ruffle	(Optional)	11 1/2 Yards
Lace for Basket		1 7/8 Yards
Backing		1 3/4 Yards
Bonded Batting		45" x 60"
Approximate Finished Size		42" x 57"

Cutting Chart

Check off and label as pieces are cut.

	Blocks	Borders
Basket Color	**Handles** ☐ One 9" Strip **Feet** ☐ One 3" Strip into (6) 3" Squares **Basket** Cut later when first handle is completed.	(5) 3 1/2" Strips
Background Color	**Handles** ☐ One 9" Strip **Sides** ☐ Two 2 5/8" Strips **Bottom** ☐ Three 5" Squares **Basket** Cut later when first handle is completed.	(6) 4 1/2" Strips
Solid Square Color	Cut later when basket block is completed.	
Fabric Ruffle		(10) 6" Strips
Backing		One Piece

Twin

Yardage Chart
Twin Quilt

	Blocks	Borders	
	Fifteen Baskets	Coverlet	Bedspread
Basket Color	1 1/8 Yards	7/8 Yards	7/8 Yards
Background Color	1 3/4 Yards	1 1/4 Yards	1 1/4 Yards
Solid Square Color	1 3/4 Yards		1 5/8 Yards
Fabric Ruffle	(Optional)	2 5/8 Yards	3 Yards
Lace for Ruffle		18 1/2 Yards	21 Yards
Lace for Basket		4 3/4 Yards	4 3/4 Yards
Backing		5 Yards	6 Yards
Bonded Batting		60" x 88"	72" x 100"
Approximate Finished Size		56" x 84"	68" x 96"

Cutting Chart
Check off and label as pieces are cut.

	Blocks	Borders	
		Coverlet	Bedspread
Basket Color	Handles ☐ Two 9" Strips Feet ☐ Two 3" Strips into (15) 3" Squares Basket Cut later when first handle is completed.	(6) 4 1/2" Strips	(6) 4 1/2" Strips
Background Color	Handles ☐ Two 9" Strips Sides ☐ Five 2 5/8" Strips Bottom ☐ One 5" Strip into (8) 5" Squares Basket Cut later when first handle is completed.	(7) 5 1/2" Strips	(7) 5 1/2" Strips
Solid Square Color	Cut later when basket block is completed.		(8) 6 1/2" Strips
Fabric Ruffle		(15) 6" Strips	(17) 6" Strips
Backing		Two Equal Pieces	Two Equal Pieces

Double

Yardage Chart
Double Quilt

	Blocks	Borders	
	Twenty Blocks	Coverlet	Bedspread
Basket Color	1 1/2 Yards	1 1/8 Yards	1 1/8 Yards
Background Color	2 1/3 Yards	1 1/2 Yards	1 1/2 Yards
Solid Square Color	2 1/4 Yards		2 Yards
Fabric Ruffle		2 3/4 Yards	3 1/8 Yards
Lace for Ruffle	(Optional)	20 Yards	22 1/3 Yards
Lace for Basket		6 1/8 Yards	6 1/8 Yards
Backing		6 Yards	6 Yards
Bonded Batting		76" x 90"	88" x 102"
Approximate Finished Size		72" x 86"	84" x 98"

Cutting Chart
Check off and label as pieces are cut.

	Blocks	Borders	
		Coverlet	Bedspread
Basket Color	**Handles** ☐ Two 9" Strips **Feet** ☐ Two 3" Strips into (20) 3" Squares **Basket** Cut later when first handle is completed.	(8) 4 1/2" Strips	(8) 4 1/2" Strips
Background Color	**Handles** ☐ Two 9" Strips **Sides** ☐ (7) 2 5/8" Strips **Bottom** ☐ Two 5" Strips into (10) 5" Squares **Basket** Cut later when first handle is completed.	(8) 5 1/2" Strips	(8) 5 1/2" Strips
Solid Square Color	Cut later when basket block is completed.		(10) 6 1/2" Strips
Fabric Ruffle		(16) 6" Strips	(18) 6" Strips
Backing		Two Equal Pieces	Two Equal Pieces

19

If you are using a dust ruffle and pillow shams on a queen size mattress, you may only want to make 20 basket blocks as in the double quilt layout and the borders as in the queen.

Yardage Chart
Queen

	Blocks	Borders	
	Twenty Four Baskets	Coverlet	Bedspread
Basket Color	1 1/2 Yards	1 1/3 Yards	1 1/3 Yards
Background Color	2 1/3 Yards	1 3/4 Yards	1 3/4 Yards
Solid Square Color	2 1/4 Yards		2 1/4 Yards
Fabric Ruffle	(Optional)	3 Yards	3 1/3 Yards
Lace for Ruffle		21 Yards	22 Yards
Lace for Basket		7 Yards	7 Yards
Backing		6 Yards	8 Yards
Bonded Batting		78" x 106"	92" x 120"
Approximate Finished Size		73" x 101"	87" x 115"

Cutting Chart
Check off and label as pieces are cut.

	Blocks	Borders	
		Coverlet	Bedspread
Basket Color	Handles ☐ Two 9" Strips Feet ☐ Two 3" Strips into (24) 3" Squares Basket Cut later when first handle is completed.	(8) 5 1/2" Strips	(8) 5 1/2" Strips
Background Color	Handles ☐ Two 9" Strips Sides ☐ Eight 2 5/8" Strips Bottom ☐ Two 5" Strips into (12) 5" Squares Basket Cut later when first handle is completed.	(9) 6 1/2" Strips	(9) 6 1/2" Strips
Solid Square Color	Cut later when basket block is completed		(10) 7 1/2" Strips
Fabric Ruffle		(17) 6" Strips	(20) 6" Strips
Backing		Two Equal Pieces	Three Equal Pieces

King Size

Yardage Chart
King Quilt

| | Blocks | Borders | |
	Thirty Baskets	Coverlet	Bedspread
Basket Color	1 3/4 Yards	1 1/2 Yards	1 1/2 Yards
Background Color	3 Yards	2 Yards	2 Yards
Solid Square Color	3 Yards		2 3/8 Yards
Fabric Ruffle	(Optional)	3 Yards	3 5/8 Yards
Lace for Ruffle	(Optional)	22 Yards	26 Yards
Lace for Basket	(Optional)	9 1/2 Yards	9 1/2 Yards
Backing		9 Yards	9 1/2 Yards
Bonded Batting		91" x 107"	106" x 121"
Approximate Finished Size		86" x 102"	101" x 116"

Cutting Chart
Check off and label as pieces are cut.

| | Blocks | Borders | |
		Coverlet	Bedspread
Basket Color	Handles ☐ Three 9" Strips Feet ☐ Three 3" Strips into (30) 3" Squares Basket Cut later when first handle is completed.	(9) 5 1/2" Strips	(9) 5 1/2" Strips
Background Color	Handles ☐ Three 9" Strips Sides ☐ Ten 2 5/8" Strips Bottom ☐ Two 5" Strips into (15) 5" Squares Basket Cut later when first handle is completed.	(10) 6 1/2" Strips	(10) 6 1/2" Strips
Solid Square Color	Cut later when basket block is completed.		(11) 7 1/2" Strips
Fabric Ruffle		(18) 6" Strips	(21) 6" Strips
Backing		3 Equal Pieces	3 Equal Pieces

Order of Basket Block Construction

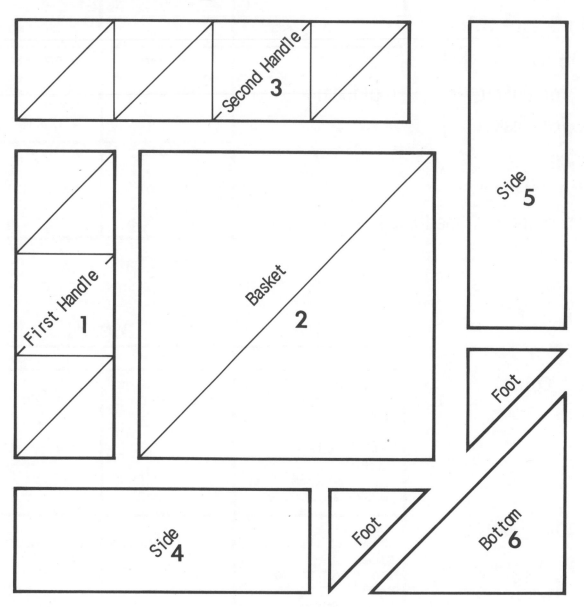

Study the names of the pieces and the order in which they are sewn together in the Basket Block.

Sewing the Basket Block

Making the Pieces for the Handle

1. Place the 9" strips of background color and basket color for the handle right sides together. Press.

2. Trim off the selvage edges on one side.

3. Draw on a 3" square grid according to your particular size quilt. Trim off any excess.

```
Baby:....(1) 9" x 15"
Lap:.....(1) 9" x 21"
Twin:....(2) 9" x 21"
    ....(1) 9" x 15"
Double:..(2) 9" x 21"
    ..(2) 9" x 15"
Queen:...(4) 9" x 21"
King:....(5) 9" x 21"
```

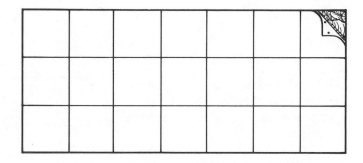

4. Draw on diagonal lines starting in the marked corner every other row.

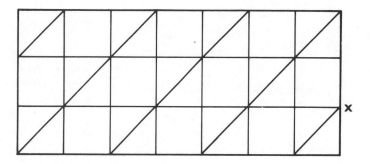

Draw on diagonal lines going in the opposite direction in the empty rows that are left.

5. Pin the two pieces together.

¼″ Seam Allowance and 15 Stitches per inch

6. Begin sewing at the point marked with an X, lining up the edge of the presser foot with the diagonal line.

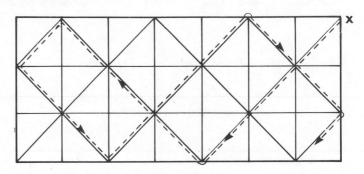

7. Continuously sew, pivoting the fabric, until you come back to the starting point.

On most quilt pieces, there is no need to remove the fabric from the sewing machine.

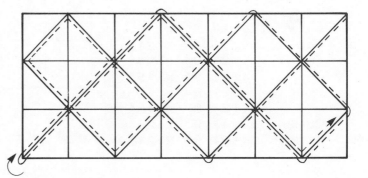

Sew on both sides of the diagonal line.

Do not backstitch.   Press.

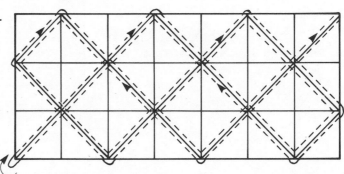

8. Lay the stitched piece on the cutting board. Line it up with the grid. With the rotary cutter and ruler, cut apart on the 3" square lines. Cut apart on the diagonal lines.

If you leave the piece laying flat on the board, you can make long diagonal cuts, and cut them apart very quickly.

A 6" x 12" ruler is handy for cutting short lines. Cut carefully and accurately.

Pressing Your Seams to the Dark Side

1. Leave your pile of pieces right on the cutting board. Do not open the pieces up. Lay the cutting board at the end of the ironing board.

2. Sort the pieces into 7 equal piles. Follow your particular quilt size for the number.

```
Baby:........4 per pile
Lap:.........6 per pile
Twin:.......15 per pile
Double:.....20 per pile
Queen:......24 per pile
King:.......30 per pile
```

3. Use steam at a cotton setting on your iron.

4. Drop the piece in the center of the ironing board with the light on the bottom.

5. Lift up the dark part and press it open and flat. Do not put down the iron.

6. Lay a second piece on top of it with light side down again. Press it open and flat.

7. Continue to press without putting the iron down; stack as you press the pieces. The dark and light will always be in the same position.

8. Lay all seven stacks in a row on your cutting board.

Making a Basket of Many Colors

1. Lay out one color in a row of seven.

2. Lay the seven blocks of the next color out on top.

3. Continue this procedure with all colors.

Making the First Handle

The pieces are laid out so that the completed basket looks like the one on the first page. If you have done any variations, pencil in your colors beside the pieces.

1. Lay out three stacks in this order next to the sewing machine.

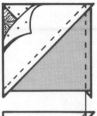

2. Flip the middle square right sides together to the first.

1/4 " seam allowance and 15 stitches per inch

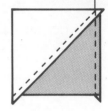

3. Anchor the two together by stitching down 1/2". Match the opposite corners of the two blocks and stretch or ease to meet.

Stitch the two together.

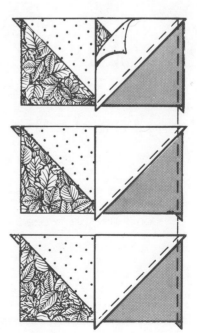

4. Flip the second middle block onto the first. Butt on these blocks by stitching continuously. Do not raise the presser foot.

5. Assembly line sew all the blocks in the first two piles in this manner.

6. Return to the first pair of blocks. Open these up.

7. Flip the third block right sides together to the pair.

8. Anchor the two, stretch or ease to meet, and stitch.

9. Continue to assembly line sew on all third blocks.

10. Lay them out in one long string on the ironing board.

11. Press across the seams, pushing the light seams to the dark side so the stitching at the point is disclosed.

12. Clip the threads holding them together.

13. Stack in one pile.

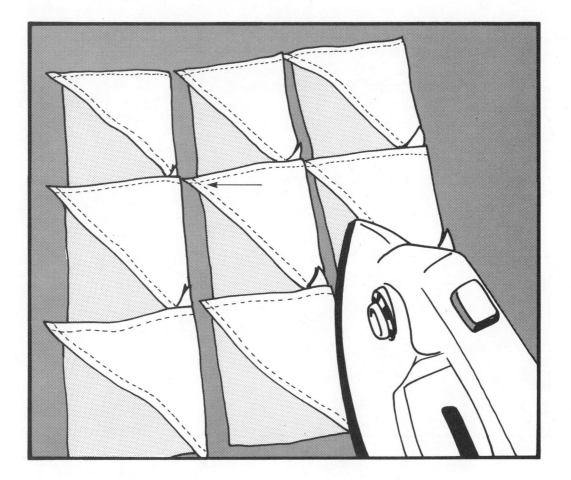

Making the Basket

1. Measure the length of several of the handles to find an approximate size.

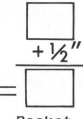

First Handle

+ 1/2"

= Basket

Add 1/2" to this figure.
(Usually between 6 1/4" – 7")

2. Cut strips that measurement x 45" of the basket color and the background color.

Cut this many strips for each quilt:

Baby:.....1/2 strip
Lap:.......1/2 strip
Twin:...1 1/2 strips
Double:.....2 strips
Queen:.......2 strip
King:...2 1/2 strips

3. Place the strips of the basket color and the background color right sides together.

4. Draw on your squares using the same measurement as your basket size.

Make this many squares for your size quilt:

Baby:..........2
Lap:............3
Twin...........8
Double:........10
Queen:.........12
King:..........15

Trim off any excess part of the strip.

5. Draw on diagonal lines in zigzag fashion.

If you are not going to add lace to your basket, skip the next page.

Inserting the Lace in the Basket (Optional):

Decide if your lace is to be enclosed within the seam or topstitched once the basket block is made. If you are going to topstitch the lace, continue on to page 32 and sew the lace on before adding the First Handle.

1. Cut the blocks apart after they are measured and marked. Leave the lace in one long piece.

2. With the background color on the bottom, enclose the lace in between the two pieces and line up the edges.

3. Assembly line sew.

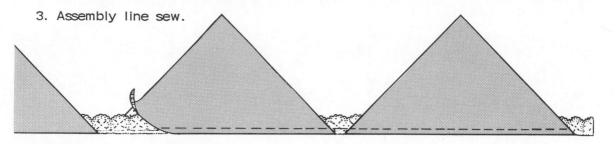

4. While the blocks are still in one long piece, press the lace to lay on the background color.

5. From the wrong side, cut apart. Trim the lace to match the corners.

6. Stack into one stack.

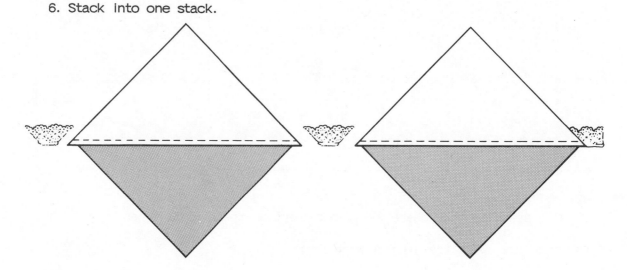

Ribbon Insertion (Optional)

1. Cut the 1/4" wide ribbon into 12" pieces.

2. With a wide eyed needle, run a piece of ribbon in from both sides. Pin the ends in place.

3. Tie in bows.

Skip to "Measuring the Basket" on page 32.

Sewing the Basket Without Lace

1. Pin the two pieces together.

2. Sew on one side of the diagonal zigzag line. Use a 1/4" seam allowance and 15 stitches per inch. Pivot at the marked points, leaving the needle in the fabric.

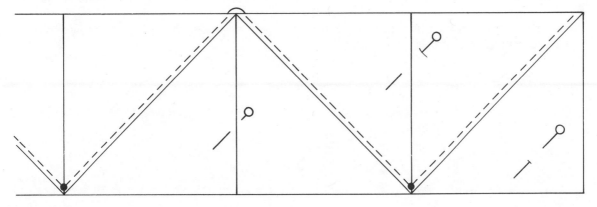

Sew to the end. Swing the fabric around and stitch along the other side of the zig zag line.

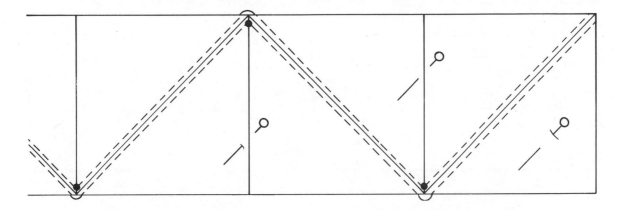

3. Cut apart on the square lines. Cut apart on the diagonal lines.

4. Press the seam toward the dark side.

5. Stack into one stack.

Measuring the Basket (With or Without Lace)

1. Measure several baskets to find an average measurement. (Generally between 6 1/4" – 7")

This measurement will be used when the sides of the basket are cut.

Adding the First Handle to the Basket

1. Lay the two stacks like this..

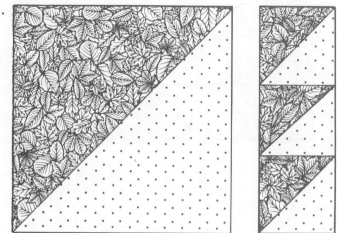

2. Flip the second one right sides together to the first.

3. Assembly line sew.

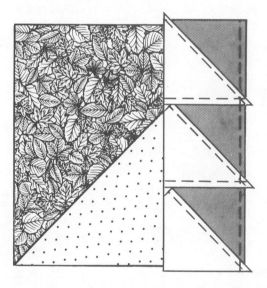

Notice how the seams are pressed and how the stitching goes through the point and not beyond.

4. Cut apart. Stack into 1 pile.

Making the Second Handle

1. Arrange the remaining four stacks of little pieces in this order.

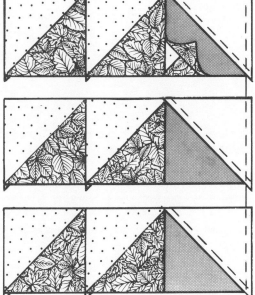

2. Flip the second block onto the first and assembly line sew.

3. Flip on the third. Assembly line sew.

4. Flip on the fourth.
Assembly line sew.

Press as described on page 29.

5. Clip the threads holding them together.

6. Stack into 1 pile.

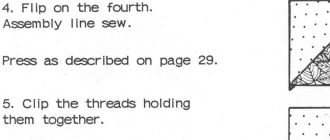

Adding the Second Handle to the Basket

1. Arrange the pieces in this order.

2. Flip the second handle onto the basket. Carefully match the seam. You may wish to pin the match point. Push the light seam toward the dark side.

3. Assembly line sew.

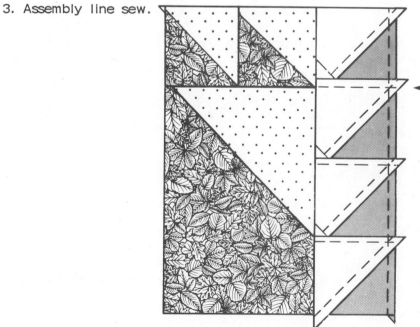

4. Clip the threads holding them together.

Adding the Foot to the Side

1. Cut the 3" squares for the feet in half on the diagonal.

2. Refer to the basket measurement found on page 32 (Usually between 6 1/4" to 7")

Cut the 2 5/8" strips into the same length. You can get between 6 and 7 per strip.

You need this many pieces for your particular size quilt:
Baby : 8
Lap : 12
Twin : 30
Double : 40
Queen : 48
King : 60

3. With half of the strips and triangles, lay them out in this order.

Use only half of the side pieces and feet.

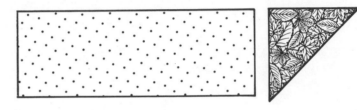

4. Flip the triangle right sides together to the strip. Allow a 1/4" tip to hang over on the bottom.

5. Assembly line sew.

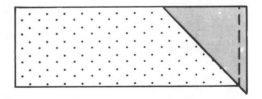

6. Press the seam to the dark side while they are in one long string.

7. Cut them apart. Stack them into one pile.

8. Lay the basket with handle out in this order with the foot strip.

9. Assembly line sew, allowing a 1/4" tip on the top and pushing the seam to the dark side.

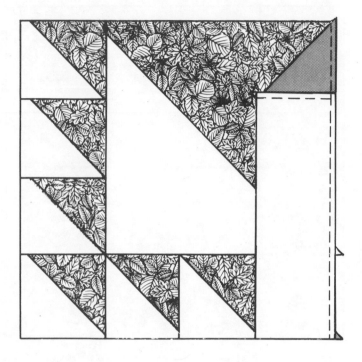

10. With the remaining half of the strips and triangles, arrange them in this manner...

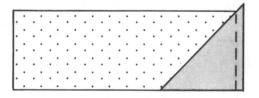

11. Assembly line sew, allowing a 1/4" tip on the top.

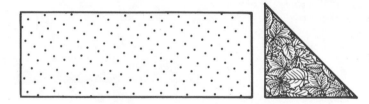

12. Press the seams to the dark side while they are in one long string.

13. Cut them apart and stack into one pile.

14. Arrange the basket with handles and last foot in this order.

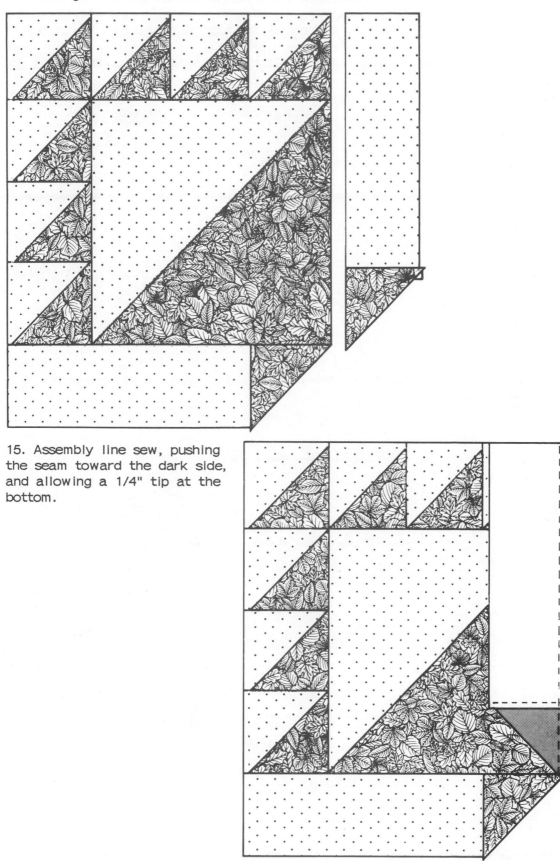

15. Assembly line sew, pushing the seam toward the dark side, and allowing a 1/4" tip at the bottom.

16. Cut the bottom 5" squares on the diagonal.

17. Assembly line sew across the bottom, allowing a 1/4" tip to hang over on both sides.

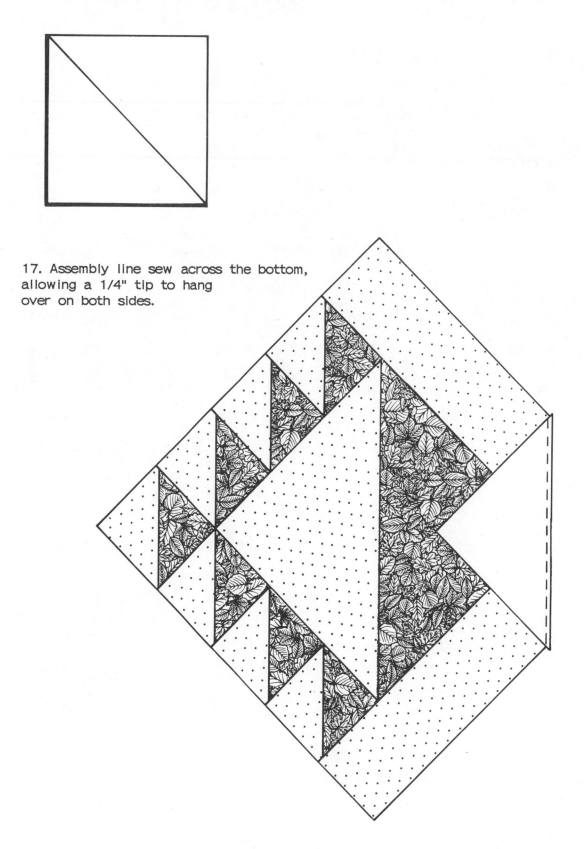

Cutting the Solid Squares

Calculating Measurements

To finish your quilt top, figure out the measurements for the solid square (SS), the corner triangles (CT), and side triangles (ST).

The example of the baby quilt shows the placement of these pieces.

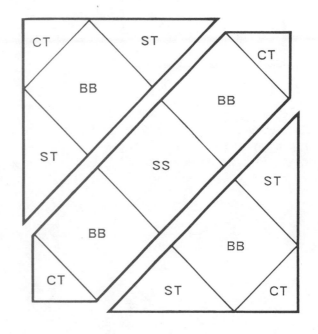

1. Solid Square: Measure the sides of several basket blocks to find an average size. They should be square.

(Approximate Example: 11")

2. Corner Triangles: Add 1" to the basket block measurement.

(Approximate Example: 12")

3. Side Triangles: Multiply the size of the basket block by 1 1/2.

(Approximate Example: 16 1/2")

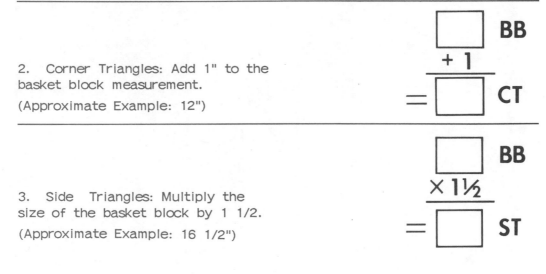

Transfer your measurements for the solid square, center triangle and side triangle to the corresponding boxes on page 41.

Cut the following pieces from the Solid Square Color. Cut the larger pieces first, and cut any smaller pieces from the scraps of the larger ones.

Cutting the Side Triangles

1. Referring to the figure found, cut squares that size.

```
Baby..............1 square
Lap...............2 squares
Twin..............3 squares
Double............4 squares
Queen.............4 squares
King..............5 squares
```

2. Layer cut these squares into fourths on the diagonals.

Cutting the Corner Triangles

1. Referring to the figure found, cut only 1 square that size regardless of the size of the quilt.

2. Cut it into fourths on the diagonals.

Cutting the Solid Squares

1. Referring to the figure found, cut squares. Use a 12" square ruler for fast, easy, and accurate cutting.

```
Baby:......................... 1 square
Lap:.......................... 2 squares
Twin:....(2) 45" strips into  8 squares
Double:..(3) 45" strips into 12 squares
Queen:...(4) 45" strips into 15 squares
King:....(5) 45" strips into 20 squares
```

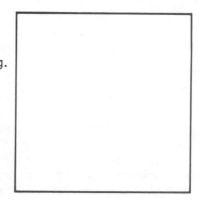

Sewing the Top Together

1. Lay out the quilt top in rows beginning with the basket blocks.   Refer to the appropriate illustration. (Pages 44–48)

```
Baby Quilt........2 across, 2 down
Lap Robe..........2 across, 3 down
Twin Quilt........3 across, 5 down
Double Quilt......4 across, 5 down
Queen Quilt.......4 across, 6 down
King Quilt........5 across, 6 down
```

2. Place a corner triangle in each corner. Place the side triangles around the outside edge, forming a straight edge. Place a solid square in rows in between the baskets.

Sewing the Quilt Top Together

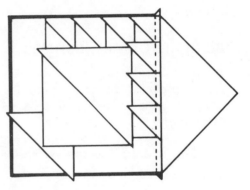

1. Flip the corner triangles right sides together to the basket blocks. Pin.

2. Assembly line sew, allowing a 1/4" tip to extend on both ends.

3. Lay the pieces back in the arrangement.

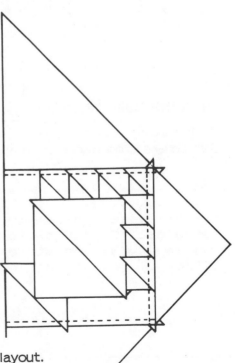

4. Starting in the upper left hand corner, flip the side triangles onto the basket in the first row. Pin, allowing a 1/4" tip to hang over on the top of the side triangles, and matching the square bottoms.

5. Stitch.

6. Lay the sewn together row back in the layout.

7. Flip right sides together and pin the second row of blocks.

8. Stitch.

9. Lay the sewn together row back in the layout.

10. Repeat this pinning, sewing, and laying out procedure until the rows are all sewn together.

11. Pin and sew the rows the opposite directions, pushing one seam one way, and one the other where the corners of the blocks join together.

Variations of Color Placement

Set baskets of the same color in diagonal rows.

For a quilt with just two different colors of baskets, arrange them in "checker board" or alternating order.

Arrange baskets of many different solid colors according to the order of their shade. Begin the row with the lightest basket on the left to the darkest basket on the right.

Variations of Basket Placement

Handles Turned To Center
Divide the quilt down the middle. Turn the handles on both sides of the middle in toward the center.

Day Bed
For a small bed that sits against the wall, turn the baskets so that the handles all point toward the wall.

Topsy Turvy Basket Quilt
Turn the handles on the top row upside down, the handles on the bottom row right side up, and the side handles toward the middle.

Baskets and Solid Blocks
Do not cut any Side Triangles or Corner Triangles but extra Solid Squares. Set all the baskets with their handles pointing to the top left hand corner of the quilt.

Baby Quilt

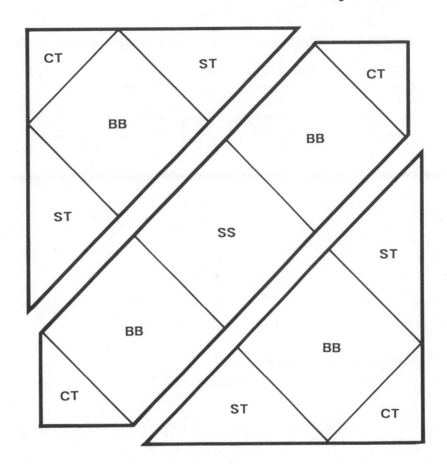

Lap Robe

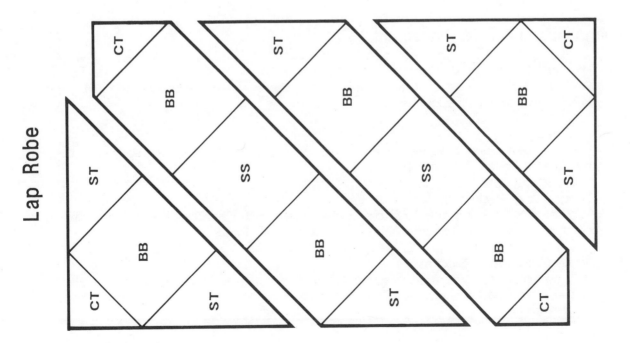

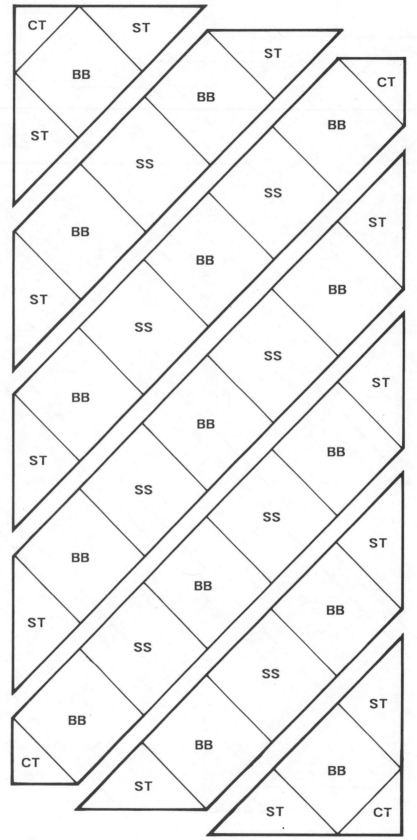

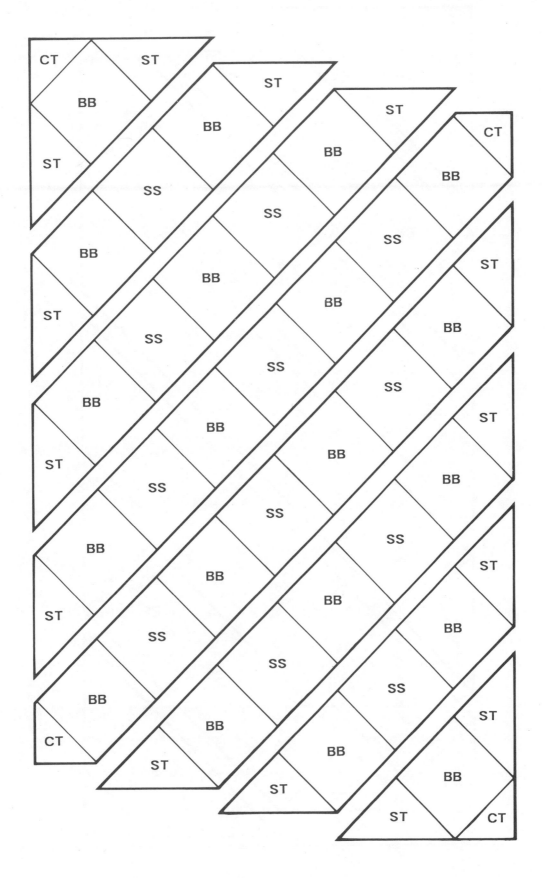

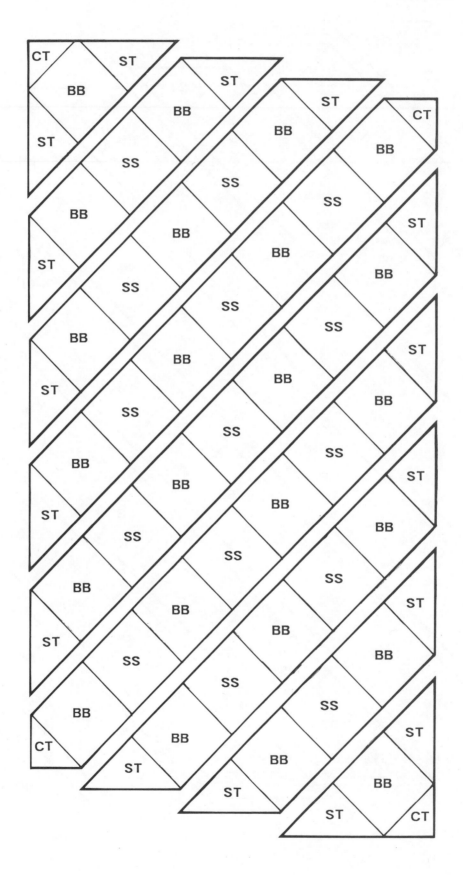

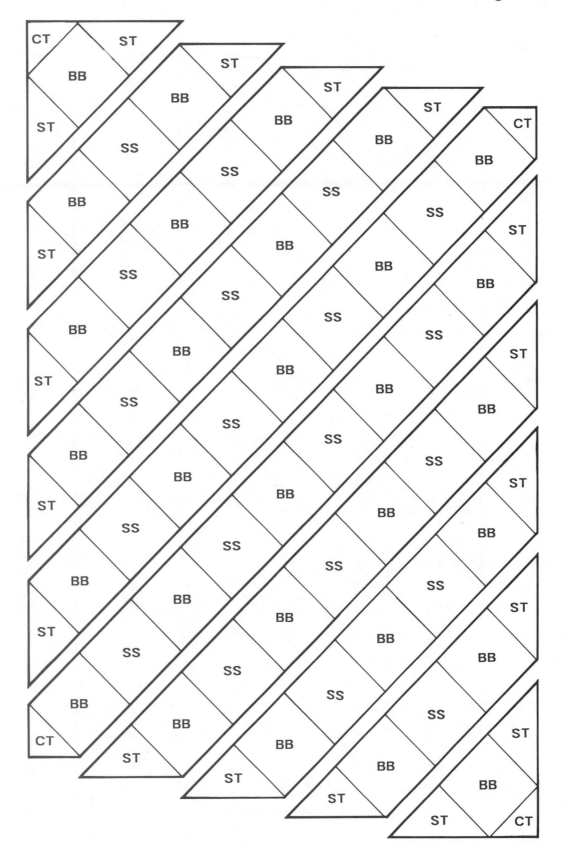

Adding the Borders to Your Quilt

Piecing the Borders

1. Follow the individual Cutting Charts for the widths of each border cut from selvage to selvage.

2. Seam the strips of each color into long pieces by flashfeeding. Lay the first strip right side up. Lay the second strip right sides to it. Backstitch, stitch the short ends together, and backstitch again.

3. Take the strip on the top and fold it so the right side is up.

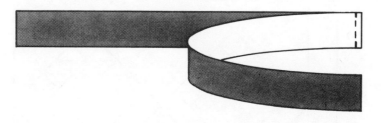

4. Place the third strip right sides to it, backstitch, stitch, and backstitch again.

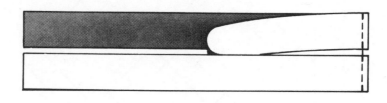

5. Continue flashfeeding all the short ends together into long pieces for each color.

6. Clip the threads holding the strips together.

Adding the Borders to the Quilt Top

1.   Measure, pin, and sew on the borders to the long sides in the First Border Color, or the narrowest border.

2. Fold the borders out flat. Trim the pieces the same length as the quilt top.

3.   Measure, pin, and sew the borders to the two short sides in the same color. Fold out flat and trim even.

4. Add on all additional borders for each color in the same manner.

Adding the Ruffle

Adding the Ruffle (Optional)

1. Follow the individual Cutting Charts for the number of 6" strips cut from selvage to selvage for the ruffle.

2. Continuously stitch the short ends together so the strips are in one long piece. Use the same methods as described when sewing the border pieces together.

3. Fold and press the long strip in half lengthwise.

To make both the long ruffle strip and the lace managable, wrap them around cardboard tubes.

4. Match the edge of the pregathered lace with the raw edges of the ruffle. Turn the narrow ends of the ruffle and the lace in 1" for a clean finished edge.

5. Begin in 1" and stitch a 1/8" seam along the edge of the pregathered lace to the end of the ruffle.

6. Position the strip and lace under the sewing needle so the lace is on the underside.

7. Set the machine with a wide zigzag and long stitch.

8. Lay a crochet thread 1/8" from the raw edge. Zigzag over the string being careful not to catch the string.

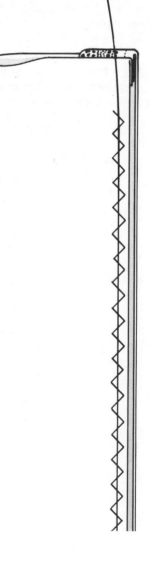

The ruffle gathering ratio is two to one. For instance, 20" of ruffle should gather up to fit into a 10" area.

9. Beginning at one corner of the quilt, measure off 10" of border and mark with a pin. Measure off 20" of ruffle with a pin.
Pull up the cord from under the zigzag at the pin mark and cut it.

10. Draw up the cord to fit the ruffle to the quilt. Space the gathers evenly.

11. Pin.

12. Continuing with the 2 to 1 ratio, draw up the cord to make the ruffle fit to the quilt. Space and pin the gathers evenly.

13. Trim off any excess ruffle and tuck the remaining 1" end into the clean fold you made at the beginning of the ruffle.

14. Stitch around the outside edge. Include the zigzag stitching in the seam allowance. Remove only the cord that shows on the right side.

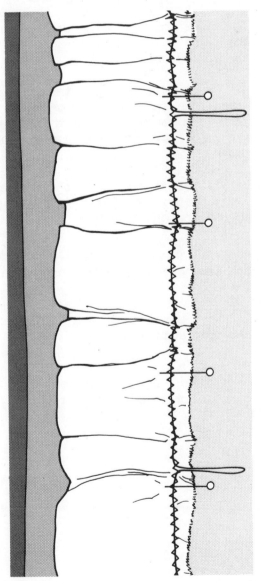

Finishing the Quilt

Adding the Backing Fabric

1. Following the individual Cutting Charts, fold and cut the backing into equal pieces.

2. Tear off the selvages and seam the backing pieces together.

3. Lay out the backing fabric on a large table or floor area with right side up.

4. Lay the quilt top on the backing fabric with right sides together. Pin. Trim away excess fabric.

5. Stitch around the four sides of the quilt, leaving a 2' opening in the middle of one long side. Do not turn the quilt right side out yet.

Piecing the Batting

The batting may need to be pieced to get the desired size.

1. Cut the batting. Butt the two edges closely together without overlapping.

2. Whipstitch the edges together with a double strand of thread. Do not pull the threads tightly as this will create a hard ridge visible on the outside of the quilt.

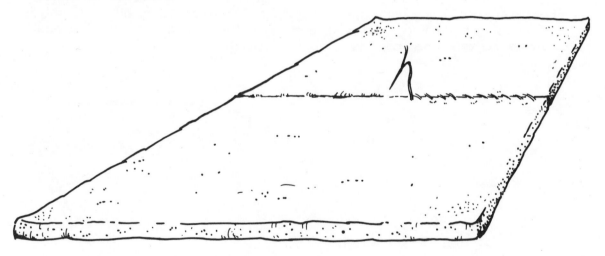

3. Lay the quilt on top of the batting. Smooth and trim the batting the same size as the quilt top.

4. (Optional) To assure that the batting stays out to the edges, quickly whipstitch the batting to the 1/4" seam allowance around the outside edge of the quilt.

Turning the Quilt Top

This part of making your quilt is particularly exciting. One person can turn the quilt alone, but it's fun to turn it into a 10-minute family or neighborhood event with three or four others. Read this whole section before beginning.

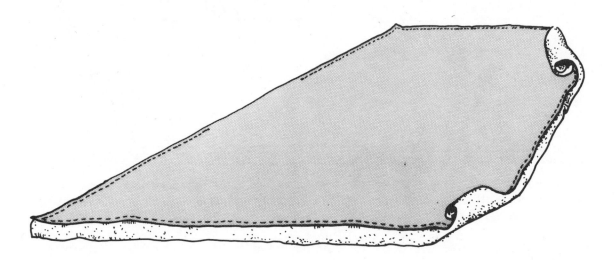

1.   If you are working with a group, station the people at the corners of the quilt. If working alone, start in one corner opposite the opening.

2.   Roll the corners and sides tightly to keep the batting in place as you roll toward the opening.

If several people are helping, all should roll toward the opening. If only one is doing the rolling, use a knee to hold down one corner while stretching over to the other corners.

3. Open up the opening over this huge wad of fabric and batting and pop the quilt right side out through the opening.

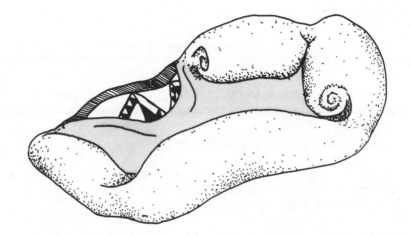

4. Unroll it right side out very carefully with the layers together.

5. Lay the quilt out flat on the floor or on a very large table. Work out all wrinkles and bumps by stationing two people opposite each other around the quilt. Each grasp the edge and tug the quilt in opposite directions.

6. You can also relocate any batting by reaching inside the quilt through the opening with a yardstick. Hold the edges and shake the batting into place if necessary.

7. Slipstitch the opening shut.

You may choose to tie your quilt down, machine quilt it with a Stitch in the Ditch technique, or use a combination of both by tying down the basket blocks and Stitching in the Ditch around the borders.

Tying the Quilt

1. Thread a large-eyed curved needle with a long strand of wool yarn, embroidery floss, or crochet thread.

If you want your square knot to show, use wool yarn. If the knot detracts from the look you want, use floss or crochet thread. For an invisible tie on the right side, pin all the points on the right side, flip the quilt to the wrong side, and tie at all pin marks.

2. With your fingers, poke in and plan where you want your ties placed. You may choose to tie just the corners of the large blocks, or tie parts of the basket also for a more dimensional look.

3. Starting in the center of the quilt and working to the outside squares, take a 1/4" stitch through all thicknesses at the points you wish to tie. Draw the needle along to each point, going in and out, and replacing the tying material as you need it.

Do not tie the borders down if you wish to Stitch in the Ditch.

4. Clip all the stitches midway.

5. Tie the stands into surgeon's square knots by taking the strand on the right and wrapping it twice. Pull the knot tight. Take the strand on the left, wrap it twice, and pull the knot twice.

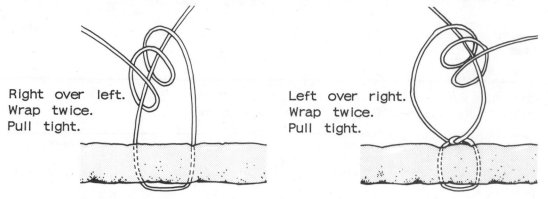

Right over left.
Wrap twice.
Pull tight.

Left over right.
Wrap twice.
Pull tight.

6. Clip the stands so they are 1/2" to 1" long.

Stitching in the Ditch

For more dimensional borders, you may choose to Stitch in the Ditch around them rather than tie them.

1. Change your stitch length to 10 stitches per inch. Match your bobbin color of thread to your backing color.

2. Change your stitch to a serpentine stitch if available. This stitch does not need to be as accurately in the ditch as the straight stitch to look attractive. Quite often, this is the stitch used by manufacturers for machine quilting.

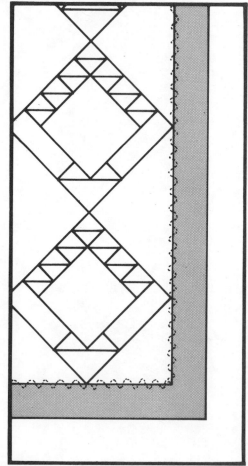

3. Pin "across the ditch" the length of the borders.

4. Place the needle in the depth of the seam and stitch. Avoid puckering on the back of the quilt by...

Running your hand underneath to feel for puckers, Grasping the quilt with your left hand above the sewing machine foot, Grasping the quilt with your right hand ten inches below the sewing machine foot, Stretching between the two as you stitch.

To further avoid puckering on the back, you may choose to use an even feed foot or walking foot available for most sewing machines.

Machine Quilt the Center of the Quilt (Optional)

1. Lay the quilt out so that it is completely smooth and flat.

2. Pin safety pins every 5" throughout the quilt away from the stitching lines.

3. Roll the quilt tightly from the outside edge in toward the middle on the diagonal. Hold this roll tightly with bicycle clips or safety pins. Put this roll into the bed of the sewing machine.

4. Using the same Stitch in the Ditch technique of stretching as described on page 57, sew down the long diagonal lines. Work from the center out to the outside edge. Unroll and roll the quilt as necessary to get all the lines stitched.

Pillows

1. Make two basket blocks following the instructions beginning on page 25.

2. Cut two pieces of bonded batting 18" square.

3. Center the baskets on the pieces of batting. Pin in place. (Optional: Machine quilt around the basket.)

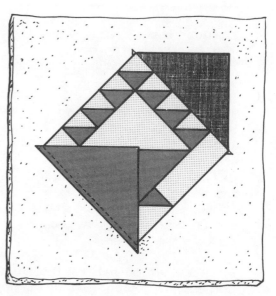

4. Cut the Solid Square Color into two 12" squares for the Corner Triangles. Cut into fourths on the diagonals.

5. Pin the Corner Triangles to two opposite corners of the baskets. Stitch in place through all thicknesses. Fold out.

6. Pin the CT to the two remaining corners. Stitch. Fold out.

7. Pin the 2 1/2" borders to two opposite sides. Trim even with the baskets. Stitch through all thicknesses. Fold out.

8. Pin, trim, and stitch on the two remaining borders. Fold out.

9. Make the ruffles and sew them to the pillow fronts following the instructions beginning on page 51.

10. Cut the backings the same size as the pillow fronts. Pin the two right sides together with the ruffles enclosed in the middle.

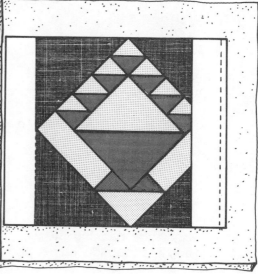

11. Stitch around the outside edges, leaving 6" openings in the middle of one side. Turn right side out.

12. Stuff firmly with shredded bonded batting, stuffing, or a pillow form.

13. Slipstitch the openings shut.

Shams

These instructions make only 1 sham for a twin sized bed. Since the larger bed sizes need two shams, double these instructions.

1. Finish the 2 basket blocks following the instructions beginning on page 25.

2. Cut the 12" square and the 16 1/2" square from the Solid Square Color into fourths on the diagonals. The smaller square makes up the four Corner Triangles, and the larger square makes up the two Side Squares. (Two are extra.)

3. Lay out the pieces in this arrangement...

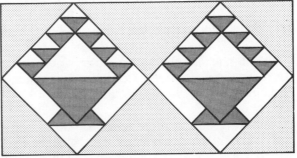

4. Flip the Corner Triangles in two opposite corners onto the basket blocks. Pin. Stitch, allowing a 1/4" tip to hang out on both sides. Lay them back in the layout.

5. Working on half of the sham at a time, pin and sew on the remaining Corner Triangle and Side Triangle.

6. Pin and sew the two halves together.

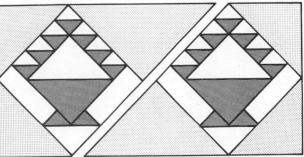

7. Center the basket patchwork on the batting. Pin. (Optional: Machine quilt around the blocks and/or baskets.)

8. Pin the borders to the two short sides. Trim. Stitch through all thicknesses. Fold out. Repeat with the two long sides. Trim any excess batting.

9. Sew on the ruffle following the instructions beginning on page 51.

10. Measure the width of the sham. Cut the backing that width by 45". (Approx. 20") Cut the backing in half down the center fold.

11. On the selvage edges, fold back a 4" hem, press, and stitch.

12. Lay one backing piece right sides together to the basket patchwork, matching the outside edges and placing the hem near the center. Lay the second backing piece on top, overlapping in the center. Pin and stitch all around the outside edge.

13. Turn right sides out.

Wallhanging

The wallhanging is one large basket using the basic illustrations and in-structions, but with larger pieces.

Making the Handle and Corner Border Patches

1. Handle: Place the 9" square basket color and background color right sides together. Draw on a 4 1/2" square grid (page 25).

2. Corner Border Patches: Place the 9" x 18" solid square color and the basket color right sides together. Draw on a 4 1/2" grid.

3. Draw on the diagonal lines and stitch (page 26.) Cut apart and press. Set the corner border patches aside.

4. Lay out the first handle and sew together (page 28).

5. Place the 11 1/2" square of the basket color and background color right sides together. Draw on a diagonal line. (Include the optional lace at this time.) Stitch. Cut apart on the diagonal line. One half will be extra (pages 30 – 32).

6. Sew the first handle to the basket (page 33).

7. Sew the second handle together (page 34) and sew it to the basket (page 35).

8. Cut the 4 1/2" square for the feet in half on the diagonal. Sew it to the ends of the side pieces (pages 36–37).

9. Sew the sides to the basket (pages 37–38).

10. Cut the 8" square bottom piece on the diagonal. Sew it to the basket (page 39).

Finishing the Basket with Machine Quilting

1. Lay the backing out flat with right sides down.

2. Center the batting on top.

3. Center the basket block in the exact middle of the backing and batting.

4. Cut the 19 3/4" square of the solid square color into fourths on the dia-gonals for corner triangles.

Machine Setting: 10 Stitches per Inch
Match the Bobbin Color to the Backing Color

5. Pin two triangles to two opposite sides of the basket through all thick-nesses. Stitch. Fold them out flat.

6. Repeat this step with the remaining two triangles.

Sewing the Borders

1. Sew a 4" strip of the basket color and the background color together 4 times, one for each side. Measure the size of the basket plus triangles and cut 4 strips that measurement.

2. Pin two border strips to two opposite sides of the basket block with the basket color strip on the inside. Stitch through all thicknesses. Fold out.

Making the Corner Patches for the Borders

3. Lay the pieces out in this arrangement.. Assembly line sew them together.

4. Sew a patch to each end of the two remaining border strips.

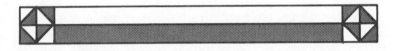

5. Carefully match and pin them to the basket. Stitch through all thicknesses. Fold them out flat.

Bringing the Backing Around to the Front

1. Trim the batting and backing evenly all around the outside edge. Trimming to an even 2 1/2" allows 1" to show on the front side.

Cut away view

2. Turn under the raw edge 1/4" and overlap it 1/4" on the quilt. Pin.

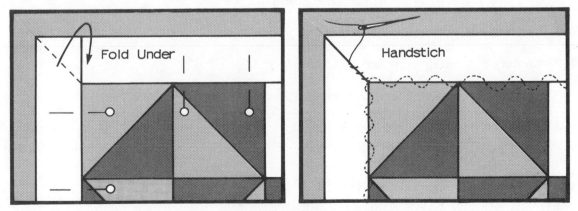

Fold Under

Handstich

3. Turn under the corners on a diagonal for a miter.

4. Machine edgestitch or hand slipstitch. Handstitch the miter.

Acknowledgements

Front Cover: Quilt by Eleanor Burns. A special thank you to Larry and Ginney Leighton of Escondido, California for the use of their historical Victorian home.

Back Cover: Quilt by Eleanor Burns. A special thank you to Grace Episcopal Church of San Marcos, California for the use of their beautiful church, currently celebrating its Centennial.

Inside Covers: Front inside cover quilt by Patricia Knoechel, Eleanor's sister. A special thank you to Lucina Heipt for the use of her home and assistance in setting up the inside cover photographs.

Appreciation to Valerie Sullivan for her inspiration, research, and assistance in making the first basket quilts.

Index

Order Information

If you do not have a fine quilt shop in your area, you may write for a complete catalog and current price list of all books and patterns published by Quilt in a Day.

Books

Quilt in a Day Log Cabin
The Sampler -- A Machine Sewn Quilt
Trio of Treasured Quilts
Lover's Knot Quilt
Amish Quilt in a Day
Irish Chain in a Day
May Basket Quilt
Schoolhouse Wallhanging
Diamond Log Cabin Tablecloth or Treeskirt
Morning Star Quilt
Trip Around the World Quilt
Friendship Quilt
Country Christmas Sewing
Bunnies and Blossoms
Creating With Color
Dresden Plate Quilt, a Simplified Method
Pineapple Quilt, a Piece of Cake

Supplies Available

Rotary Cutters
Rotary Replacement Blades
Cutting Mats with Grids
6" x 6" Mini Rulers
6" x 12" Rulers
6" x 24" Rulers
12 1/2" x 12 1/2" Square Up Ruler
Quilter's Pins
Magnetic Pin Holder
Magnetic Seam Guides
Curved Needles

Patterns and Other Projects

Dresden Placemats and Tea Cozy
Log Cabin Wreath
Log Cabin Christmas Tree
Easy Radiant Star Wallhanging
Flying Geese Quilt
May Basket Quilt
Angel of Antiquity
Diamond Vest and Strip Vest
Country Patchwork Dress

Videos for Rent or Purchase

Log Cabin Quilt
Bear's Paw Quilt
Monkey Wrench Quilt
Ohio Star Quilt
Lover's Knot Quilt
Amish Quilt
Irish Chain Quilt
May Basket Quilt
Schoolhouse Wallhanging
Diamond Log Cabin
Morning Star Quilt
Trip Around the World
Friendship Quilt
Block Party Series #1 and #2
Radiant Star Wallhanging
and more!

If you are ever in Southern California, San Diego county, drop by and visit the Quilt in a Day Center. Our quilt shop and classroom is located in the La Costa Meadows Business Park. Write ahead for a current class schedule and map.

Quilt in a Day
1955 Diamond Street, San Marcos, California 92069
Phone: 1-800- U2 KWILT(1-800-825-9458) Information Line: 1-619-591-0081